Spirit of God:
the Healing One

Jason Wagner

Table of Contents

Chapter 1: Faith, Healing, and Forgiveness: Lessons from the Journey

In my journey of experiencing God's miraculous healing in my life, I have learned to apply spiritual principles for healing. In times past, I spoke the word of God and meditated on Genesis 2:7, believing that God's breath of life could heal me. I want to emphasize to you that it's the speaking the word of God, drawing strength from it, and maintaining faith that got me through the battles. Later, I sought medical help, when I discerned that it was also necessary.

What I would like to write about at the onset, however, is something that probably none of us would want to confess to another. That is the role that unforgiveness sometimes can play in hindering our healings. Simply said, unforgiveness can act as a spiritual block to healing. I believe this is why, after many years of learning about the miraculous, I have now written this book and am sharing my experience with you, because unforgiveness towards my ex-wife prevented my healing from sciatic nerve pain. Reconciliation and forgiveness, you will learn, were key to my road to recovery. I really want to appeal to you, as you read this, Here are just a few truths we will look at:

Insights from Apostle Jason's Experience

✠ Believers are called to actively practice the teachings of the Word, seeking God directly for their healing instead of depending solely on the faith of others.

✠ Illness and suffering do not originate from God; rather, they are attacks from the enemy.

✠ God's primary method of imparting wisdom and guidance is through His Word.

✠ Applying spiritual principles such as speaking God's Word, meditating on scripture, and maintaining unwavering faith were essential for my journey to healing.

✠ Medical intervention was also sought when discernment indicated it was needed.

I want to get personal in this, because with the afflictions that came in my life, when I was a baby Christian, I struggled with these questions. Below are three key questions and answers that are addressed within the pages of this healing book, providing clarity on foundational topics for anyone seeking divine healing:

1. Can evangelists or others pray for my healing, or must I receive it myself?
2. Is sickness a way God teaches or disciplines people?
3. What is the meaning of Jehovah Rapha?

Looking back, I am grateful for every lesson I learned and for the opportunity to share my testimony. My name, Jason, means "the healing one," and it inspires me to help others discover how to receive healing for themselves. I want people to know that faith—even as small as a mustard seed—can activate God's healing power, and that being a doer of the word, seeking God, and forgiving others are all crucial to experiencing the fullness of what Christ accomplished for us. I am so blessed to share these stories and to encourage others to claim God's healing and trust Him as Jehovah Rapha, the Lord our healer.

As I look back, I am deeply grateful to share my personal journey in this book—especially how God's miraculous power helped me overcome life-threatening blood clots in my lungs. It is my hope that as I recount these experiences, you will find encouragement to seek God for yourself and trust Him for your own healing.

I give God all the glory for what he did for me and what he showed me along the way, as I through faith and speaking God's breath into myself, and later with medical intervention, experienced the multifaceted approach to healing that the Lord did in my life.

As I mentioned, I experienced significant health issues, including blood clots in the lungs, which I first encountered after COVID-19. Later I was faced with a more severe recurrence of this condition, along with sciatic nerve pain that lasted for about a year and a half.

I had to face and work through that, and I discovered through a book called 'Our God-Breathed!' by John R. Rice, of the breath of God and I just took it so seriously that if He breathes into me, why not? Number one, you've got to believe. I just want to talk about what I dealt with as that's what inspired me to deal with healing. Reflecting on Genesis, I remembered how God said, "Let us make man in our image," and breathed life into him. Inspired by this, I took the Bible and prayed for God's breath to fill me. Day by day, I felt my strength returning—I started eating more, taking natural remedies and supplements like vitamin C, and gradually regained my stamina. When I could barely walk before, I began to move around more and eventually returned to work. As I healed, I no longer needed that support and was able to let them go. However, about five years later, the blood clots in my lungs returned even more severely, leaving me exhausted and struggling to breathe.

I went to work, trying to function, and driving as best as I could. Someone said, "You need to go to the doctors." but I was thinking, "I'm healed by the Lord.", I'm not saying to ignore the doctors but at some point, you have to believe God. So, I finally went to urgent care. Urgent care checked me out. They said, "Something's wrong. We're going to send you over to the hospital at Redlands Community in California." So, I went there. They immediately did a checkup on me, an MRI. They saw that there were blood clots in my lungs. I said, "Oh, not again." Long story short, they did a procedure. They took a tube and ran it up me and sucked all the blood clots out and I was doing a lot better. This happened back in March of this year, 2025, and I wasn't taking any medicine to thin the blood, so they were building up, the blood clots, and I guess I had them in my legs, too, but they resolved everything.

I began standing on the word declaring, "I'm the healed of the Lord" and with the things I'm doing now - I'm working out, I'm going to the gym, I'm walking more, I'm doing things even at this age, that I should be doing that will help make me stronger, in these past 9 months. However, the foremost principle is declaring God's Word with faith, which Jesus powerfully demonstrated throughout His ministry—even before He went to the cross. The scripture referenced is:

Matthew 4:23 – "Jesus went into all Galilee, teaching in their synagogues, and preaching the gospel of the kingdom, and healing all manner of sicknesses and matter of disease among the people."

So, when some claim Jesus doesn't heal everyone, remember—His healing is accessible to all who reach out in faith. Every person who encountered Him found wholeness, and at the cross He opened the door for anyone to receive salvation, healing, and deliverance. The invitation remains: believe in what Christ accomplished at Calvary and experience the fullness of God's redemptive power in your own life. I will make that invitation available to you on these pages. The key to this is to understand the totality of what Christ accomplished at the cross. Salvation is much more than just a ticket to heaven.

Salvation is a powerful, all-encompassing word in the Gospel that brings together every act and process of redemption. It means complete deliverance—not just from sin, but also from dangers, troubles, sickness, and even poverty. Salvation offers freedom from every aspect of sin, including the old nature—what the Bible calls the "old man"—and from the grip of the enemy. If we were still held captive by sin or Satan in any way, it wouldn't be true deliverance at all.

Now that includes everything that could or has happened to you and to me. I just shared with you what happened to me. Reflect on that for a moment and re-read this a few times. Take a few days and really process what that means for you and I as redeemed sons and daughters of God. When we experience sickness, we have to recognize that the Lord did not create it. Instead, he has allowed satan to manufacture it and use it to war on the saints as a result of Adam's transgression. What is clear is that the redemptive process is absolutely a part of the salvation experience that the believer enters upon regeneration through becoming born-again. You can clearly see the love of God for mankind through this generous offering by God, of a solution to the problem of the devil, by enabling us to be delivered from the enemy and his trickery. So, when we say we are saved, we are referring to being delivered from sin AND sickness! In this particular instance the Lord redeemed my physical body and as part of the process of healing, gave me a wonderful education on healing and deliverance.

He took your sins. He took your pain. He took all

your sickness. He took all the stuff that you're dealing with, that you need to be delivered from. He took it all. When we receive what He did at the cross, it doesn't stop there. He didn't just die. We know He rose again. So now this becomes alive in you. Your faith becomes alive because you start by hearing the word of God. You speak the word of God, and it becomes alive and it brings forth healing. It brings forth finances. If you declare these things with conviction, they will come to life. I'm certain of this, even though we all face moments of doubt. Do your best to set doubt aside, because when we believe without wavering, we can receive the blessings God intends for us.

Of course, it has to be in alignment with Him. So, we need to be in alignment with Him when we want something. I want to deal with the time that I was like, "How come I didn't get healed? It's been, you know, like three weeks." I couldn't understand. I had this sciatic nerve problem. I hurt myself when I worked for the phone company and I didn't deal with it. The doctor said, "You're going to need surgery." I was like, "Well, no, I'm believing God for a healing." I had every faith person I knew praying for me and I had to walk it out for about a year and a half. I was taking 800 ibuprofen three times a day. I couldn't walk, and I couldn't stand without any uncomfortability. But I went to this church. In fact, I lived down the street from the Rock church in San Bernardino. And this lady says to me, "You have unforgiveness in your heart."

So, if you don't know anything about unforgiveness then this book is really for you. You see, it's really a simple concept -sometimes trespasses can keep you from getting healed. If you have unforgiveness toward God, toward someone, or even toward yourself, those things can stand in the way of your healing. That's exactly what was happening to me. My ex-wife, well, I had unforgiveness towards her because she left me and the three kids. So, I reached out to her, and together, we reconciled and faced that pain. I asked her, "Can you forgive me for what I've done?" She did the same, and though we never got back together, the bottom line is, we made peace. She later passed away at 50 years old, in 2023. I'll never forget that date—9/11—just like the tragedy in New York, it's etched deep in my memory. But when that unforgiveness was finally dealt with, that's when the healing began..

Well, that's my testimony. This book is the fruit of it and as I close this chapter, let me encourage you: healing isn't just a physical journey, it's deeply spiritual and emotional. Sometimes, the breakthrough you're longing for is waiting on the other side of forgiveness. When you let go of past hurts, when you release what you've been holding onto, you create space for God's healing power to move in your life. The process may not always be easy, and the restoration may not look like what you imagined, but the freedom and peace that comes with true reconciliation is undeniable. I invite you to take that step—whether it's forgiving someone else, yourself, or even God. As you do, trust that healing will begin to flow, and you'll experience the fullness of God's redeeming love in ways you never thought possible. Let forgiveness open the door to your miracle.

Chapter 2: Walking in the Reality of Divine Healing

The Foundation and Process of Receiving Healing

Negative self-talk and doubt can hinder God's work, as God is a gentleman and requires an invitation through faith and His word. Healing is a finished work of Christ at the cross, and believers must apply it to their lives by faith and speaking His word. Faith is not based on feelings or physical sensations but on the truth of God's word. To receive healing, you must first believe that Jesus Christ is Jehovah Rapha, your healer, and that you can go to Him for healing. This belief is the foundation of faith. You then need to speak God's word and claim your healing, even if you don't feel or see it immediately. It's about receiving what God has already provided through His finished work at the cross, rather than trying to 'get' something.

Healing can manifest suddenly or gradually over time, as seen in Daniel's three weeks of persistent prayer. The key is to maintain faith and continue believing God's word, regardless of immediate results. Spiritual illiteracy—failing to know or read God's word—can hinder this process, as it prevents you from knowing what to speak or how to respond, and limits God's ability to guide you toward His intended purpose.

Your words are critical in the healing process. Speaking God's word and affirmations of faith invites Him to act, while negative or doubting statements close the door to His intervention. Co-laboring with God means partnering with Him: He provides the Spirit, power, and anointing, but you must participate by using faith, declaring His word, and obeying His guidance. The authority for your healing comes from Jesus Christ's finished work at the cross—He bore your infirmities, making salvation, healing, and deliverance available to all who believe. When seeking healing, focus on God's promises, not on how you feel.

So, then what? If we aren't healed within a certain timeframe, it's important to remember that the process is closely tied to our relationship with Christ and our spiritual understanding. Knowing the word is knowing Him—His ways, His patterns, and how He's working through us. When we neglect the Bible and remain spiritually illiterate, it limits how God can communicate and guide us toward the healing and breakthrough He desires for us. God wants to co-labor with us, working through us as His vessel. Think of it like a glove and a hand: we are the glove, but without God—the hand inside—the glove can't move or fulfill its purpose. It's His Spirit that gives us boldness, power, and anointing to step into the assignments He's placed before us. Too often, we allow doubt to shortchange what God wants to do, but instead, we should declare, "In Christ, I can do all things," remembering Ephesians 1:3: "All things are already given to us."

Everything in heaven is available to us here on earth—right now. The key isn't to strive to get something, but to simply receive what God has already made available. Receiving comes through speaking by faith, just as God spoke creation into existence. Our faith-filled words activate God's promises in our lives, but we must know His word to know what to declare and what He's calling us to do. This understanding leads us to walk in our healing.

Take Daniel's story, for instance: his prayers took three weeks before the angel arrived with the answer, affirming that his prayers had already been approved. This reveals a principle—those who truly seek God, who are anointed and attentive to His voice, can access His power from within. It's not something we look for externally; it dwells inside us when we are spirit-filled. When we declare God's word in faith, we set the stage for His power to move.

If healing or breakthrough hasn't manifested within three weeks, consider what Daniel's experience teaches: sometimes there is an appointed time for answers to come. The number 21 in Hebrew represents "the appointed time." In these waiting periods, it's crucial to be discerning about what teachings we receive and to stay connected with seasoned ministers who genuinely love God and His people. Above all, love for people is vital, it's the heart of true ministry. If you find yourself stuck, revisit Hosea 4:6: "My people perish for lack of knowledge." Continue to seek wisdom, meditate on

God's word, and trust that as you grow in knowledge and faith, the fullness of your healing will follow.

Receiving your healing begins with unwavering belief in the Healer, Jehovah Rapha—Jesus Christ. You must approach Him with faith, trusting that He is able and willing to restore you. This is where YOUR testimony begins: as you praise and glorify God for His touch, your healing starts to manifest, even if you don't immediately feel or see the change. Sometimes healing happens instantly, other times it unfolds over days or weeks, but faith is always the foundation. Let Daniel's 3 weeks be the litmus test for your own healing. God is actively providing the opportunity for healing because He alone is the Healer, and you must hold onto that truth for every part of your being, from head to toe.

Next, consider the woman with the issue of blood—her expectancy fueled her faith as she reached out to touch Jesus' garment, believing she would be made whole. This same expectancy is essential when you come before God, knowing that He has already made healing available. I cannot emphasize that enough. Salvation, healing, and deliverance are not distant promises; they are present realities to be received and applied to your life. When you trust God as your Healer, you'll experience His shalom and peace as healing takes root in your body. Stand firm on His word, praise Him, and let your testimony glorify Him, just as those healed in scripture did—returning to give God the glory.

It's important to recognize the power of your words in the process of receiving healing. Jesus asked the man at the gate beautiful, "What do you want me to do?"—reminding us that belief and expectation are crucial. If you speak doubt or negativity, you hinder God's work, but when you align your confession with His promises, you invite Him to act on your behalf. God knows your needs, but He waits for you to invite Him through faith-filled words. Speak His word, declare your healing, and trust that He is working for you. This is how you receive: by believing, declaring, and inviting God to move as you walk out your healing in faith.

Let me take you to Proverbs 4:20-22 for a moment. It says, "Those that find my words", you have to catch that! Find my words. That means you have to seek them out, pursue them diligently and when you discover these words, stand firm on them, because they are health to your flesh. Nowhere in the Bible does it say, "Check your body to see if you're healed." Healing comes as you go, along your journey. It's your faith that gives you access to what God is doing in your life. But you must trust His perfect timing, because sometimes He's working on something within you. I'll be the first to admit, there was a season—a year and a half—where I didn't realize I was harboring unforgiveness. But thank God I was listening for His voice, and He showed me exactly what I needed to do. That testimony alone should encourage you to examine yourself right now. Ask, "Lord, what do I need to change? Am I declaring the things of the Lord so I can receive healing?" This is a teaching I'm passionate about.

Remember Mark 4:24, we have to attend. What we hear, what we focus on. What we hear is what we attune to. If we're hearing bad teaching, then all of our problems become that thing: bad teaching. When we pay too much attention to certain trends or media that lack Christian values, then we get off track. The world's wisdom can also easily distract us. Ecclesiastes 12:12 reminds us that you can read countless books and have all the knowledge, but even a prestigious education can't compare to the wisdom found in a single chapter of the Bible.

So, what I'm saying to you is this. You got to watch what you're hearing. Watch what you're looking at and attending to. If you want more healing, you got to read the scriptures and have a seasoned minister in your life, or your favorite ministry you see online or read good books that teach Christ's truths. Get the revelation of what God has for you. That is where you get the 100-fold. You have to meditate on it and see what that is. When you meditate on the Word, you'll get the revelation. So, if you're not getting healed, there's something you're not doing. It's that simple. Police yourself. Go to God. If the healing is for you, it's in you. You see, you're a new creature. We're all new creatures who are in Christ. God's not getting anybody sick to teach them. He doesn't teach like that. Usually when you're sick, you've allowed the enemy to convince you that this is coming onto you.

As I reflect on my journey and pen these thoughts, I realize how deeply they connect to everything I have learned in my faith walk towards healing. So, I want to emphasize the importance of knowing God's word—not just as information, but as the foundation for our relationship with Christ and our spiritual understanding. My testimony about dealing with aches and pains, once I learned some of these truths, inspired me to reject what the enemy tried to put on me and that is a practical example of what it means to stand firm in faith and not consent to defeat. Just as I've learned to say, "No, I don't receive—I don't consent," I encourage you to recognize that the enemy will back down when you stand on God's promises and refuse to accept anything contrary to His word.

Throughout this chapter, I've shown that healing isn't something we have to chase externally; it's already been given to us through Christ. It's our responsibility to reach within, declare God's truth, and walk out our healing by faith, trusting His perfect timing. Whether it's immediate or takes longer—like my own experience with unforgiveness—what matters is that we remain obedient and sensitive to God's voice, allowing Him to reveal and address anything that may hinder our breakthrough.

Everything I've shared, from Daniel's story and the appointed time for answers, to the necessity of meditating on scripture and guarding what we hear, comes down to this: your healing is a present reality. Like the woman with the issue of blood, expectancy and faith fuel your journey. Even when attacks come, I've learned to declare, "It's not mine in the name of Jesus—I'm going to overcome this." I'm living proof that standing on the finished work of Christ and claiming His promises will bring victory. Whether healing arrives instantly or unfolds over time, God is always faithful to His word.

So, whatever comes to you, I want you to remember that we are new creations in Christ. God isn't using sickness to teach us; He's provided healing as our inheritance. Speak life, stand firm, and walk out your healing in faith—knowing that God is with you every step of the way. His power is available right now, and your testimony will glorify Him as you receive all that He has already made possible through Jesus.

As I close this chapter, I want to decree a prayer over you, and I encourage you to make this prayer your own. Don't just listen—repeat these words aloud and let faith rise within you. Personalize each declaration, speaking life and blessing over yourself and those you love. Let your heart believe and your mouth confess what God has already accomplished for you at the cross. Here's how you can do it:

"Lord, I come before You right now, speaking words of life over myself and my loved ones. I declare that I am healed by the Lord, that I am blessed, and that I am joined together with those You have ordained for my life and relationships. Father, I ask in the mighty name of

Jesus that You release finances, healing, and restoration into my life—from the top of my head to the soles of my feet. I declare that the enemy cannot come against what You

have put together in my relationships, and that our bond will be strengthened and not easily broken. Strengthen the ministry You've given me, Lord, and provide for the vision You have placed in my heart. I believe provision is coming my way. For anyone, including myself, dealing with sickness or lack, I command every detrimental condition to be uprooted in the name of Jesus. I declare wholeness over my life. I choose to receive all that You have done at the cross, knowing it is already finished and paved for me. I speak out in faith, trusting You for a quick work in my body, my finances, and my relationships, right now, in the mighty name of Jesus. Amen."

Let these words become your daily confession. Speak them boldly, believe them deeply, and watch God move powerfully in every area of your life. Your testimony will glorify Him as you walk in the blessings He has already provided. Hallelujah.

Chapter 3: Biblical Healing Scriptures: A Journey through Old and New Testaments

Discovering the Continuity of God's Healing Power for Faith, Healing, and Restoration

Introduction: Importance of Healing in Scripture

From Genesis to Revelation, the Bible is filled with promises and demonstrations of God's healing power. Healing is not just a peripheral theme; it is woven through the tapestry of Scripture as a testament to God's compassion, faithfulness, and desire for His people to walk in wholeness. Let's explore how biblical healing unfolds across the Old and New Testaments, and how these truths can impact your life today.

Old Testament Foundations: Genesis to Deuteronomy

✠ Genesis 22:17 – The Blessing Begins: God promises Abraham, "I will surely bless you and make your descendants as numerous as the stars... and through your offspring all nations on earth will be blessed." This foundational blessing encompasses not only prosperity and protection but also the promise of divine health and restoration.

✠ Exodus 15:26 – God Our Healer: The Lord says, "I am the Lord who heals you." This is the first explicit declaration of God as healer, linking obedience to His commands with the promise of physical well-being.

✠ Leviticus 14 – Cleansing and Restoration: God provides detailed instructions for the cleansing of lepers, symbolizing both physical healing and spiritual restoration. Healing in Scripture is always holistic—body, soul, and spirit.

✠ Numbers 21:4-9 – The Bronze Serpent: When the Israelites were plagued by serpents, God instructed Moses to lift up a bronze serpent; those who looked to it were healed. This act of faith pointed forward to Christ, who would be lifted up for our healing and salvation.

✠ Deuteronomy – Healing Relief and Obedience: Throughout Deuteronomy, God reiterates that obedience brings blessing, including health and relief from affliction. "The Lord will keep you free from every disease..." (Deuteronomy 7:15).

Historical Books and Psalms: Heart, Strength, and Restoration

✠ Music and Peace (David and Saul): When Saul was tormented, David played the harp and God's presence brought relief and peace (1 Samuel 16:23). Worship and music are powerful instruments of healing for the mind and heart.

✠ Psalms – Healing and Wholeness: The Psalms are filled with references to God's healing power. "He forgives all your sins and heals all your diseases" (Psalm 103:2-3); "The Lord sustains them on their sickbed and restores them from their bed of illness" (Psalm 41:3).

✠ 2 Kings – Renewal and Obedience: The stories of Elisha and Elijah illustrate God's miraculous intervention and healing, underscoring the importance of faith and obedience.

✠ 1 Chronicles 4:10 – Jabez's Prayer: Jabez prayed for blessing, enlargement, and protection, and God granted his request. This demonstrates that heartfelt prayer can bring healing and transformation.

✠ 2 Chronicles 7:14 – Healing the Land: "If my people... will humble themselves and pray... I will heal their land." National and personal healing are connected to repentance and seeking God's face.

✠ Job's Restoration: After suffering loss and sickness, Job's restoration came when he prayed for his friends and trusted God's sovereignty. God "restored his fortunes and gave him twice as much as he had before" (Job 42:10).

Prophets: Isaiah, Jeremiah, Ezekiel, Hosea, and Malachi

✠ Isaiah 53:5 – By His Stripes: The Messiah is prophesied to bear our griefs and carry our sorrows; "by His stripes we are healed." This is a cornerstone for Christian faith in divine healing.

✠ Jeremiah – Restoration and Healing: "I will restore you to health and heal your wounds," declares the Lord (Jeremiah 30:17). God's heart is always toward restoration.Ezekiel – Deliverance and New

Heart: God promises deliverance from captivity and a new spirit within His people (Ezekiel 36:26).

✠   Hosea 6:1-2 – Healing and Revival: "He will heal us... He will bind up our wounds." God's desire is not only to forgive but to revive and restore.

✠   Malachi 4:2 – Healing in His Wings: "But for you who revere my name, the sun of righteousness will rise with healing in its wings." God's healing is for all who honor Him.

The Gospels: Jesus' Healing Ministry

✠   Jesus Heals All: The Gospels are saturated with Jesus healing the sick, casting out demons, and re-storing broken lives (see Matthew 8:16-17; Mark 1:34; Luke 4:40). His miracles confirm that God's kingdom brings wholeness.

✠   Compassion and Authority: Jesus healed out of compassion and with authority, demonstrating that God's will is health and life for His children.

✠   Faith's Role: Again and again, Jesus affirms, "Your faith has made you well" (Matthew 9:22; Mark 10:52), showing the importance of believing and receiving.

Acts and the Early Church: Apostolic Healing and Miracles

✠   Acts – Miracles Continue: The apostles, filled with the Holy Spirit, continue the healing ministry of Jesus (Acts 3:1-10; 5:12-16; 9:32-35). Miracles, signs, and wonders confirm the message of the gospel.

✠ Community of Faith: Healing often takes place in the context of prayer, unity, and faith-filled community.

Pauline Epistles: Spiritual Gifts, Wholeness, and Application

✠ Spiritual Gifts: Paul teaches that gifts of healing are part of the Spirit's work in the church (1 Corinthians 12:9). Healing is available for today!

✠ Wholeness in Christ: The epistles underline that God desires for you to be "sanctified wholly—spirit, soul, and body" (1 Thessalonians 5:23).

✠ James 5:14-16 – Prayer for the Sick: "Is anyone among you sick? Let them call the elders... the prayer of faith will make the sick person well." Confession, prayer, and anointing with oil are practical, biblical steps for receiving healing.

Revelation: Healing of the Nations

✠ Revelation 22:2: In the new creation, "the leaves of the tree are for the healing of the nations." God's ultimate plan is for complete and eternal healing for all who belong to Him.

Practical Application: Standing on the Word, Faith in Action

These scriptures are not just ancient promises—they

are living truths for you today. Meditate on them, speak them out, and stand in faith. Healing flows as you apply the Word, surrender your heart, and trust in God's timing and method. Remember, healing is not only for your body but for your mind, emotions, relationships, and the land you dwell in.

Let worship, praise, and prayer become your daily practice. Invite the presence of God—just as David's music brought peace to Saul, allow His presence to bring healing to every area of your life. Seek out community, ask for prayer, and don't hesitate to reach out to seasoned believers and leaders for support.

God's healing power is continuous—from Genesis to Revelation, He is unchanging, faithful, and present to restore you. God is ready and willing to bring healing and restoration to your life today! As we've explored throughout this chapter how God's healing power is available and active from Genesis to Revelation, let us now come together in prayer, trusting Him to bring restoration and wholeness to every area of our lives.

Just as we see in the story of Naaman at the gate of Bethesda from 2 Kings 5:1-19, God's healing power is not limited by status, wealth, or the severity of our condition. Naaman, a mighty general, found himself desperate and humbled by leprosy—a disease that stripped away not only his health but also his pride. It was through the humble faith of his Hebrew handmaiden, the guidance of God's prophet, and obedience to a simple command that Naaman found restoration. Seven times he dipped into the Jordan, and though he struggled with pride and offense, it was his surrender to God's way that brought complete healing; his skin was restored like that of a child. This account echoes the examples we've explored throughout this chapter: God's healing is available, active, and often found when we surrender our expectations and trust in His timing and method. Naaman's journey reminds us that healing comes not from our own efforts or resources, but through humble faith, obedience, and reliance on God's Word. Just as the prophet refused earthly reward, pointing all glory back to the Lord, so too must we recognize that true wholeness and restoration are gifts from God alone.

Let Naaman's story inspire you as we approach God in prayer. Whether you're facing sickness, emotional pain, or a situation that feels hopeless, remember: God is ready and willing to restore you. As you trust Him, stand on His promises, and invite His presence into every area of your life, may you experience the victory and wholeness that only He can give. Now, let us join together in faith and prayer, believing for healing, deliverance, and newness of life—just as God transformed Naaman, He desires to do the same for you today.

In the mighty name of Jesus, we bring every need, every burden, and every desire for healing before the Lord. Father, for those who are facing challenges, who feel in need of deliverance or rescue, we ask You to be their defender and their Savior. You are the God who fights our battles and brings victory when we call upon Your name.

We stand on Your Word and declare that, by the stripes of Jesus, healing is available and active for every sickness and every affliction. For those experiencing illness, we pray for Your restoring power to bring wholeness to body, mind, and spirit. For those facing adversity or oppression, we ask for Your protection—a shield of faith surrounding every heart and life. Lord, for those seeking salvation, may they call upon You and receive a new heart and a renewed spirit, set free to walk with You in wholeness and peace and we anchor ourselves in Your promises, believing that Your healing is not limited by circumstance or condition. May every person standing on these Scriptures experience the fullness of Your restoration—healing in every area of life and the victory that comes from trusting in Your unfailing love. We pray all these things in the precious name of Jesus. Amen

Chapter 4: Natural and Supernatural Healing: God's Provision for Wholeness

Introduction: Embracing Both Paths to Healing

I want to share a message about both natural healing and spiritual healing—how God uses both practical wisdom and His miraculous power to make us whole. This chapter will reveal to you the tools in both the spirit and in the natural, that the Lord has given us to be the healed of God.

Firstly, we can look at some simple, practical things you can do for your body to support healing, but never forget—it's the supernatural, the very presence of God, that brings true miracles, wholeness, and lasting freedom. When you experience God's touch, you don't have to keep struggling with the same pain or illness.

Stretching and Exercise: Simple Steps for Relief

There are exercises I've learned that have truly helped me—simple stretches I've shared with others, and they've found relief, too. Before we dive into the scriptures, let me give you a practical example. One stretch I call the "Oh God Effect": Take your right or left arm, reach it behind your neck or shoulder—however far you can comfortably—and hold it for about 30 seconds. You'll feel the stretch through your neck, shoulder, and arm. Switch arms and repeat. This is an easy way to relieve tension and promote healing in those areas.

This helps loosen up the neck and shoulders. If you have shoulder problems, don't hesitate to ask for prayer as well. For tightness in your knees or legs, just lie on your bed and gently pull one knee up toward your body and hold it—no need to get on the floor if that's too difficult. You'll often feel a little pop or click, and things start to feel easier. Repeat with the other leg. I picked up some of these stretches from PBS health programs, and they really work to get the blood flowing, especially when your joints are stiff or sore.

Try these stretches in the morning when you get up, or at night when you're winding down and your body aches. Even if you just slept wrong or feel sore, these small things can help your body heal naturally.

Nutrition and Wisdom: God's Natural Remedies

Nutrition is another key—God's given us so many remedies in nature. For example, I've found Renavive helps with kidney stones which develop with the building up of citric acid in the body. Tart cherries are great for arthritis and gout, blueberries sharpen the mind, and broccoli is full of potassium. Of course, moderation is important—too much milk, soda, or alcohol can lead to kidney stones, so wisdom is needed in what we take in.

There are also wonderful spices that help with inflammation and blood pressure. I've started using turmeric for pain and cinnamon for blood pressure, and they've been a blessing. There's so much information out there, but these are things I know work because I've experienced them. Praise God for providing these natural resources for our healing!

But there comes a time when natural remedies aren't enough—when the pain is too great, or the diagnosis is too severe. That's when we need Jesus to intercede. When doctors have done all they can, and the enemy tries to bring discouragement, we can take our stand in God and resist the enemy's attacks.

Faith and Authority: Claiming Your Healing

In the book of John, right after Jesus turned water into wine—a miracle so pure and holy it didn't lead to drunkenness but revealed the glory of God—His disciples believed in Him because they saw God's power. Believe, and you will receive! Take authority in faith and declare, "This is my healing!"

Don't claim the sickness as your own—claim healing as your inheritance. If changes are needed, God will show you, whether it's cutting back on sugar or soda, or making wiser choices about what you eat and drink. That's just good sense, and God will give you the strength for each step.

Remember, your body is the temple of the Holy Spirit. Take care of it—exercise, walk, ride a bike, and make wise choices. You don't have to have a gym membership; just move your body and treat it well. Drink more water, juice, and foods that cleanse and nourish your body.

Miracles: The Power of Supernatural Healing

Jesus performed miracles everywhere He went, delivering people from sickness and disease. Sometimes, only the supernatural power of God can bring the breakthrough. In John 6:2, multitudes followed Jesus because they saw His miracles—and God is still working miracles today!

Think about the Azusa Street Revival of 1906 in Los Angeles—people were healed, delivered, and set free. Miracles happened as God poured out His Spirit, and that same move of God is coming again. In these last days, God is pouring out His Spirit on all flesh—young and old, men and women, everyone who believes. Healings are coming faster than ever before. God wants to touch you right now—He is not a "someday" God, but a "right now" God! He wants to heal you, fill you, and bless you today. All you have to do is ask!

God's Names: Provider, Healer, and Peace

He is Jehovah Jireh—your provider; Jehovah Rapha—your healer; and Jehovah Shalom—your peace. Some of you may need deliverance in your mind, not just your body. Receive His peace today, and let Him calm your thoughts and restore you completely. God's peace can drive out headaches, anxiety, and unrest.

Look for my next book in 2026, where we'll go even deeper into healing and deliverance for the whole person—body, soul, and spirit. This chapter lays the foundation for understanding how God cares for the complete person and provides both natural and supernatural means for our healing. As we have seen, food and drink play a big role in this, just as they did in the life of Jesus, especially in His most critical moments.

Standing on God's Word: Spiritual Authority

Let's look at Luke 4, where Jesus, right after forty days of fasting—a season of change—was tempted by Satan. The enemy questioned Him, and Jesus answered with the Word. When Satan or his minions attack you with doubt, fear, or condemnation, answer with God's promises! The Word of God never comes back empty (Isaiah 55:11).

Keep speaking the Word over your life and situation. Just like your mom or grandma always had the last word, let God's Word have the last word in your life, and you'll see the enemy flee.

After His temptation, Jesus stepped into His ministry and declared in Luke 4:18 the authority we have to receive and declare healing. You have the name of Jesus, His precious blood, and the power of the Holy Spirit—resurrection power—living inside you! Let these truths rise up in you, speak them over your life, and watch as God brings healing, deliverance, and breakthrough.

Take five minutes to praise God right now, and let His Spirit quicken your body. You have all the tools you need: the name, the blood, and the power. Hallelujah!

Receiving Wholeness in Every Area

In summary, God provides for our healing through both natural means—like nutrition, exercise, and wise choices—and supernatural power made available through faith in Christ. When you combine practical wisdom with a strong spiritual foundation, you open yourself to complete wholeness. God desires for you to prosper in your body, soul, and spirit. No matter what you're facing today, remember that healing and deliverance are part of your inheritance as a child of God. Stand on His Word, use the tools He's given you, and trust Him for every breakthrough. God's provision is enough for every challenge—receive it now, and step into His fullness and freedom.

Chapter 5: Experiencing Healing and Deliverance Through Faith

Standing on God's Promises for Restoration

Healing and Deliverance in the New Testament

We have come to the end of this book, which is a pocket sized teach-up designed to be taken with you wherever you go, as both your devotional to affirm that you are the healed of God, but also as a resource to bring God's healing power to everyone whom you come into contact with. The Lord has given us everything we need, as his hands and feet, the New Testament church, which is the only divine authority on the earth mandated to speak for Him and move like Him. We see right away in the synoptic gospels that healing and deliverance are found throughout the New Testament churches' inception. This is especially highlighted in Luke 4:18. In this passage, Jesus declared, "The Spirit of the Lord is upon me because he has anointed me to preach the gospel to the poor. He has sent me to heal the broken-hearted." The crucial word in this verse is "heal," which encompasses restoring sight to the blind as well as setting at liberty those who are bruised or oppressed. This passage emphasizes that healing is available for those who are brokenhearted, and that deliverance is promised to captives—meaning anyone in need of freedom, whether they are bound by sin, afflicted by infirmity, or hindered by other struggles in life. The Bible further assures us, "He whom the Son sets free is free indeed," so anyone who desires freedom can receive it through faith in Jesus. This verse does not imply that a person is demon-possessed; rather, it teaches that believers can experience oppression by the devil. However, if we choose to trust God and rely on His promises, we can be set free from any form of oppression. The setting free of captives serves as a powerful symbol of deliverance from both physical and spiritual bondage, whether it stems from sin or from Satan, but through faith in the Lord Jesus Christ, complete freedom is made possible. As I said in the opening, by standing firmly on His Word, believers can experience true freedom, victory, and deliverance in their lives. So, I now want to leave you with a few key points to bear in mind as you release your faith into the world, as the chosen vessel fit for the Masters use. These are some final thoughts to take with you and exercise as you become skillful in the Word and mature in your faith! Remember, this is only the first book of many that will be made available to you in the coming years. So, let the healing begin!

The Power of Worship and Speaking Life

You may often hear televangelists or speakers discuss the concept of a healing anointing, and that is truly a wonderful gift. If you are Spirit-filled, I encourage you to pray in tongues, because many believers testify to the tremendous power that comes from praying in the Spirit. Additionally, worship music is widely believed to usher in the presence of God, which can create an at-mosphere for miracles. While it is true that Jesus never

had a praise band accompany Him, you can still worship Him and sense His presence in your own way, and
when you do so, you may notice things begin to change
and work for good. However, I want to invite you into
a more personal and intimate space—whether you are
one-on-one with your family, standing beside a loved
one in a hospital room, comforting a sick employee, or
visiting your grandmother or cousin who lives alone.
The Word of the Lord, as promised in Isaiah 55:11,
never returns void. This means that when you stand on
Scripture and declare God's promises, those words will
accomplish what God intends—they never come back
empty or unfulfilled. Here are two important principles
to remember whenever you minister to someone: first,
decree and speak life, because your words have the
power to change someone's destiny; and second, declare
life over them, because Proverbs 18:21 teaches that "the
power of life and death is in the tongue." You have the
authority to speak healing and restoration over others.

Faith in Action: Laying Hands and Believing

What I would personally do in these situations where
you have an opportunity to bring healing and deliverance on the scene, is to lay hands on those who are sick
or in need. The Bible instructs us to lay hands on the
sick so that they might recover. You perform this act
by faith, and it does not require you to be an apostle,
prophet, or any special title—just a believer who acts in
faith. What kind of faith do you need for this? It doesn't
have to be an enormous or overwhelming amount of

faith; in fact, Jesus taught that even faith as small as a mustard seed is enough. The reason for this is found in 1 Corinthians 12:8-11, where Paul describes nine gifts of the Spirit, which are divine gifts given by God that come into operation once your faith matures and reaches fullness. Your faith can grow stronger as you spend time studying the Word of God, praying in tongues, and praising Him with sincerity. Even if you only have a little faith, simply do what you know to do, especially if you feel led by God in that moment. The most important thing is to be guided by God and to listen for what He is saying to you. If you stand on His Word—as Jesus taught in Matthew 7—you are building your house on a solid rock foundation. The house in this teaching represents you, and the rock represents someone who not only hears the Word but acts on it. After the rain falls and storms come, if you are still standing strong, it is a sign that you have received healing and are firmly rooted in God's promises.

Encouragement for Everyday Challenges

If you, or someone you know is facing financial difficulties or any other challenging situation, remember that the Word of God is incredibly powerful—never underestimate its effectiveness. Teach people in your life; Aunt Sue, grandma, Uncle Moe, or anyone you encounter, to have even a little faith. What example did Jesus give us? Even when people only had a small measure of faith, He still called them healed and restored. Colossians 1:13 proclaims, "He has delivered us from the power of darkness and translated us into the kingdom of His dear Son." When we consider who the dear Son is, we recognize Him as Jesus Christ, the Anointed One, our Savior and Redeemer. Praise God for His goodness and mercy.

He has brought deliverance to us through His divine anointing and through the abiding presence of His Spirit. The key is that we don't need to pray for more faith but only activate the faith we have.

Standing Firm in God's Presence

When we remain in His presence and walk in the fullness of His anointing, we can stand firm in faith. The enemy is powerless before God and cannot prevail against Him. Whenever you are in God's presence, surrounded by His anointing, and standing on His Word, the enemy has no chance—not in this world and not in the realm of the Spirit. Life overcomes death and destruction which come from the enemy.

Freedom from Every Addiction

This is the key takeaway in this book. Take this thought with you; Deliverance is available for you—God has the power to set you free from every addiction. Whether you or someone you know struggles with cigarettes, alcohol, pornography, or any other stronghold, God's deliverance is for you. The key is to become "addicted to Jesus"—to dedicate yourself wholly and completely to the Lord. When you surrender in this way, God will deliver you and set you free. If you find yourself repeatedly returning to an addiction, it is a sign that you need God's intervention and deliverance, because it can be extremely difficult to quit on your own. With God, all things are possible, and He will set you free from addiction when you put your trust in Him and allow Him to work in your life. When you align yourself with God and join Him in faith, He will break every chain, for "he whom the Son sets free is free indeed."

Hearing God's Voice and Receiving Revelation

Here's a valuable lesson I learned to couple with the freedom that I just mentioned: How can you be sure that God is speaking to you? According to 1 Kings 19:12, God's voice is often a still, small voice, just as the prophet Elijah experienced. He did not hear God in the loud wind, the fire, or the rain, but rather in a gentle whisper. This quiet voice can be compared to a small child softly whispering in your ear. If you desire to hear from the Lord, speak to Him, ask Him to respond, and listen carefully with your heart—then you will notice that gentle, still voice. Make a habit of practicing this sensitivity to God's voice. Also, pray every day and learn to pray in tongues. If you want to receive the gift of tongues, seek out a mature believer who can lay hands on you and pray for you—this is a significant step because the gift of tongues brings spiritual power and growth. The next step is to diligently study the Word of God and strive to understand it. If God cannot communicate with you on a mature level, you may not fully comprehend what He is saying or what He wants to do in your life. God can speak in simple, childlike ways, but true healing often requires spiritual power and understanding. Many of the greatest ministers only received their healing after they grew in their understanding of the Word and learned how to apply it. It is essential to learn how to hear God's voice so you can receive revelation from Him. Once you have received revelation, begin teaching and praying for others—start ministering to those around you so that you can receive further revelation and power to pray for their needs. Even if they are on the deathbed, don't hesitate to pray for that person. Start right now and watch what God will do in your life. Praise is also a key element of spiritual breakthrough; God inhabits the praises of His people, and that brings His glory into your circumstances. Through praise, you will witness miracles—such as cancer disappearing, backs straightening, and broken limbs being restored. No matter how long it has taken for you to reach your current situation, continue to believe God, and know what God says—open your Bible, stand on His promises, and begin to believe for your healing and breakthrough.

Conclusion

As you come to the end of this book, my heart is full of gratitude for the journey we have taken together. I want to remind you that no matter what challenges or obstacles you face—be it sickness, financial hardship, addiction, or moments when God's voice seems quiet—His presence remains steadfast and His promises are unchanging. If you have even a mustard seed of faith, you possess all you need to receive healing, deliverance, and every good thing God desires for you. Don't underestimate the power of God's Word, the gift of prayer, or the life-changing presence that comes when you praise Him with sincerity.

Remember, deliverance and freedom are not reserved for a select few, but are available to all who trust in Jesus and yield their hearts to Him. God's Spirit is always with you, ready to guide, restore, and empower you for every circumstance. If you ever feel weak, discouraged, or uncertain, stand firm on the rock of His Word—just as Jesus taught—knowing that storms may come, but God's love will hold you secure.

My hope is that these pages have encouraged you to grow in faith, to listen for God's gentle whisper, to lay hands on those in need, and to boldly believe for miracles in your life and the lives of others. May you walk in the fullness of God's anointing, experience the joy of His deliverance, and live each day in the confidence that whom the Son sets free is truly free indeed. Amen.

Jason Wagner was born in Hollywood at General Hospital, a city renowned for its vibrant culture and creative spirit. From a young age, Jason felt a strong calling to serve God and his community, which led him to begin his ministry journey in the local church. Starting as an usher, he quickly embraced greater responsibilities, becoming an ordained minister and youth pastor from 1991 to 2000. His deep passion for pastoral care and mentoring led him to continue as an ordained minister, focusing on providing spiritual guidance and support from 2000 through 2022.

Throughout his calling, Jason has invested over sixteen years ministering in Hollywood, impacting countless lives with his dedication and compassion. He also played a pivotal role in singles ministry for five years, helping individuals cultivate faith, community, and purpose during transitional seasons of life. Jason's heart for service is evident in his commitment to both young people and adults, always striving to bring hope and healing through the message of Christ.

In 2023, Jason transitioned into prophetic and apostolic ministry, embracing a new season of spiritual leadership. With decades of experience in pastoral care and a passion for empowering others, he now serves as a prophetic voice and apostolic leader, seeking to equip the next generation and bring about spiritual transformation. His journey reflects unwavering faith, resilience, and a lifelong commitment to advancing God's kingdom.